Abracadabra
Violin

Book 1 – Violin part

Peter Davey

A & C Black · London

Contents

Clown dance 4
Bobby Shafto 5
Au clair de la lune 6

First finger

One finger dance 7
Spinning wheel 7
Seagull 7

Second finger

Frère Jacques 8
Hot cross buns 8
Waltz 9
Suo-gân 9
Windmill song 9

Third finger

Clown dance 10
Little bird 10
Andrew mine, Jasper mine 11
Summer shine 11
Rolling 12
When the saints go marching in 12
Hush-a-bye baby 13
Twinkle, twinkle little star 13

Fourth finger

Hello morning 14
Shepherds' hey 14
Au clair de la lune 14
Big Ben 15
Hot cross buns 16
Oranges and lemons 16
I'm the urban spaceman 16
London Bridge 17
Scale of D 17

E string

Little bird 18
Twinkle, twinkle little star 18
Little donkey 19
Frère Jacques 20
Winds through the olive trees 20
Baa, baa, black sheep 21
Clown dance 21
Scale of A 21
Baa, baa, black sheep 22
Off to France in the morning 22

London's burning 23
Can-can 23
Hickory dickory dock 23
Kum ba yah 24
Three blind mice 24
The first Nowell 25
Puff the magic dragon 26
An Eriskay love-lilt 26
Funny dance 27
Supercalifragilisticexpialidocious 27

New position, second finger

Happy birthday 28
Thank U very much 28
Jingle bells 29
Here we go round the mulberry bush 29
Folk waltz 30
Away in a manger 30
Morningtown ride 31
Last of the summer wine 31
While shepherds watched their
    flocks by night 32
Unto us a boy is born 32
Theme from the ninth symphony 33
Morning has broken 33

G string

Scale of G 34
God save The Queen 34
Plaisir d'amour 35
Deck the hall 35
Sing a song of sixpence 36
Theme from 'Swallow Suite' 37
My love is like a red, red rose 38
The grand old Duke of York 39
Give me oil in my lamp 39
Theme from 'Bridges of Paris' 40

New position, third finger

Brother James' air 40
Hornpipe 41
O soldier, soldier 42
Scale of A 42
Scottish medley 43
French folk medley 44
The birdcatcher's song 45
St Anthony chorale 46

Acknowledgements 47
Index of titles 48

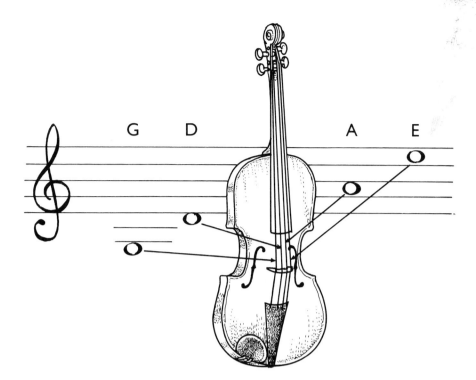

Introduction

'Abracadabra Violin' is based on a simple principle; that pupils will learn to play more easily and effectively tunes which are already known. In particular, instrumental technique and ear training will be encouraged by the use of tunes which pupil and teacher can sing.

This book differs from traditional violin tutors in its flexibility. It contains a refreshing selection of carefully-graded tunes covering each aspect of technique. However, there is a minimum of didactic text; no-one can learn to play a stringed instrument from written instructions, no matter how sound the theory behind them. Individual teachers should find nothing here to contradict their own approach, nor any general assumptions made about their pupils' rates of progress.

Thus the fourth finger is introduced as an option (in brackets). The pupil may use the alternative open string at first, then come back to the tune when other aspects of technique have improved enough to allow full concentration on the unfamiliar fingering. Bowing indications are minimal to encourage pupils to take the initiative; further markings can be pencilled in as required.

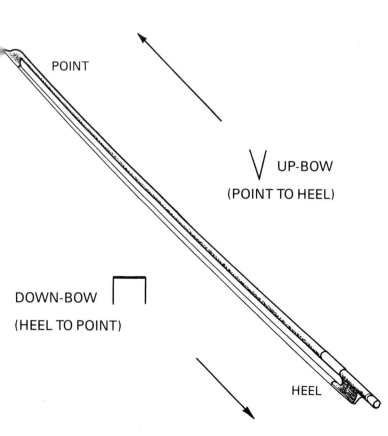

POINT

∨ UP-BOW
(POINT TO HEEL)

DOWN-BOW ⊓
(HEEL TO POINT)

HEEL

ISBN 0 7136 5543 7

First published 1985 by
A & C Black (Publishers) Ltd
35 Bedford Row, London WC1R 4JH
© 1985 A & C Black (Publishers) Ltd
Reprinted 1986, 1987, 1990, 1991, 1993, 1995, 1997, 1998.

4

Clown dance

traditional French

You play your open D string. Play these bars four times:

Your teacher plays this:

Bobby Shafto

traditional

You play D and A:

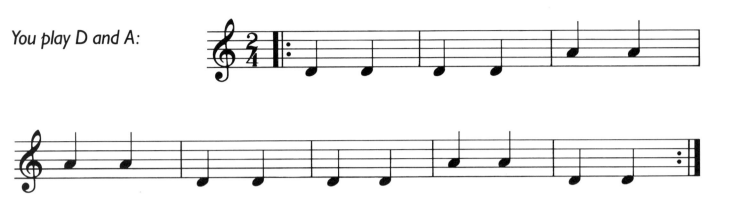

Your teacher plays this:

Bob – by Shaf – to's gone to sea, ___ sil – ver buc – kles on his knee, ___

He'll come back and mar – ry me, ___ bon – ny Bob – by Shaf – to.

Bob – by Shaf – to's bright and fair, comb – ing down his yel – low hair,

He's my own for e – ver more, bon – ny Bob – by Shaf – to.

Au clair de la lune

traditional French

You play:

Teacher:

One finger dance

P. D.

Spinning wheel

P. D.

Seagull

P. D.

These tunes are played on the D and A strings. If you can learn them by heart,
you could try them on the A and E strings, using the same fingering.

Frère Jacques

traditional French

Play these notes on the D string while your teacher plays the tune:

Teacher:

Hot cross buns

traditional

Hot   cross   buns,   hot   cross   buns,

One   a   pen – ny,   two   a   pen – ny,   hot   cross   buns.

Waltz

P. D.

Suo~gân

words: Percy Dearmer
music: traditional Welsh

Win - ter creeps, Na - ture sleeps, Birds are gone, Flowers are none.

Windmill song

P. D.

10

Clown dance

traditional French

You could compose a tune of your own using all three fingers on one string.

Little bird

German folk song

Andrew mine, Jasper mine

words: C. K. Offer
music: Moravian carol

An - drew mine, Jas - per mine, Ti - mo - thy and A - bel,

Hur - ry to Beth - le - hem, to the com - mon sta - ble.

There you'll find a ba - by small, sleep - ing in a swad - dling shawl;

On your way, on your way, to our Sa - viour born to - day.

Summer shine

P. D.

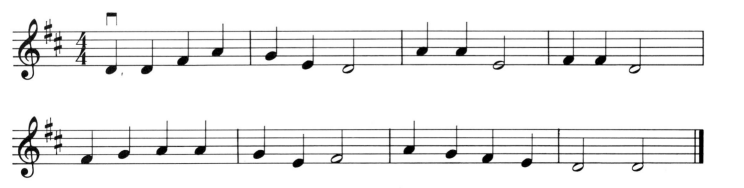

12

Rolling

P. D.

When the saints go marching in

spiritual

Oh, when the saints go march - ing in,

Oh, when the saints go march - ing in,

I want to be with - in that num - ber _____

_____ When the saints go march - ing in.

Hush~a~bye baby

traditional

Hush - a - bye ba - by on the tree top,

When the wind blows the cra - dle will rock.

When the bough breaks the cra - dle will fall,

Down will come ba - by, cra - dle and all.

Twinkle, twinkle little star

words: Jane Taylor
music: traditional

Twin - kle, twin - kle lit - tle star. How I won - der

what you are. Up a - bove the world so high,

like a dia - mond in the sky. Twin - kle, twin - kle

lit - tle star. How I won - der what you are.

Hello morning

P. D.

Shepherds' hey

Morris dance

Au clair de la lune

traditional French

This is the teacher's part from page 6. Now you try:

Now play it starting on G. You can play the whole tune this way:

Big Ben

anonymous

Big Ben all day long goes

Ding, Dong, Ding, Dong. Small clocks on the wall say

Tick, tock, Tick, tock, Tick, tock, Tick, tock. Bu - sy lit - tle

watch - es whis - per Tick - a - tock - a, Tick - a - tock - a, Tick - a - tock - a, Tick.

16

Hot cross buns

traditional

Turn to page 8 and play the tune again. Then try it like this:

Oranges and lemons

traditional

Or - an-ges   and   le - mons Say   the   bells   of   St   Cle - ment's. You

owe   me   five   far - things   Say   the   bells   of   St   Mar - tin's.

I'm the urban spaceman

Neil Innes

I'm   the   ur - ban   space - man,   ba - by,   I've   got   speed, ___

___   I've   got   ev - 'ry - thing   I   need.

I'm   the   ur - ban   space - man,   ba - by,   I   can   fly. ___

I'm a su - per - so - nic _____ guy.

I don't need plea - sure, I don't feel

pain, If you were to knock me down I'd just get up a -

- gain, I'm the ur - ban space - man, I've got hairs on my

chest, I ne - ver get de - pressed.

London Bridge

traditional

Lon - don Bridge is fal - ling down, Fal - ling down, fal - ling down.

Lon - don Bridge is fal - ling down, My fair la - dy.

SCALE OF D

Little bird

German folk tune

Twinkle, twinkle little star

words: Jane Taylor
music: traditional

Little donkey

Eric Boswell

Frère Jacques

traditional French

Frè - re   Jac - ques,   Frè - re   Jac - ques,

dor - mez - vous?   Dor - mez - vous?   Son - nez les ma - ti - nes!

Son - nez les ma - ti - nes!   Ding,   Dang,   Dong!   Ding,   Dang,   Dong!

Winds through the olive trees

traditional French

Winds   through the   o - live trees   soft - ly   did   blow

Round   lit - tle   Beth - le - hem,   long,   long   a - go.

Sheep   on   the   hill - side   lay   white   as   the   snow,

Shep - herds   were   watch - ing   them,   long, long   a - go.

Baa, baa, black sheep

traditional

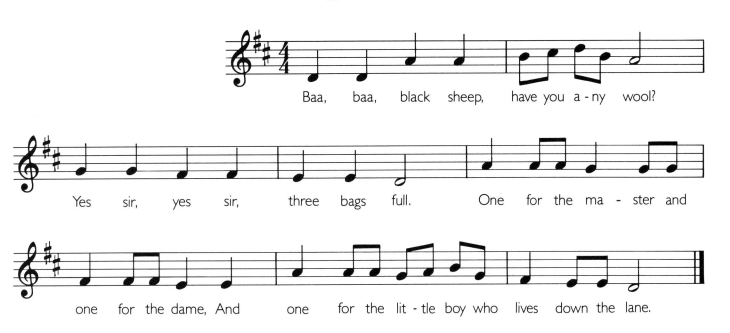

Baa, baa, black sheep, have you a-ny wool?

Yes sir, yes sir, three bags full. One for the ma-ster and

one for the dame, And one for the lit-tle boy who lives down the lane.

Clown dance

traditional French

SCALE OF A

Baa, baa, black sheep

traditional

Off to France in the morning

Peter Davey

London's burning

traditional

Lon - don's burn - ing, Lon - don's burn - ing, Fetch the en - gines, fetch the

en - gines. Fire! Fire! Fire! Fire! Pour on wa - ter, pour on wa - ter.

Can~can

Offenbach

Hickory dickory dock

traditional

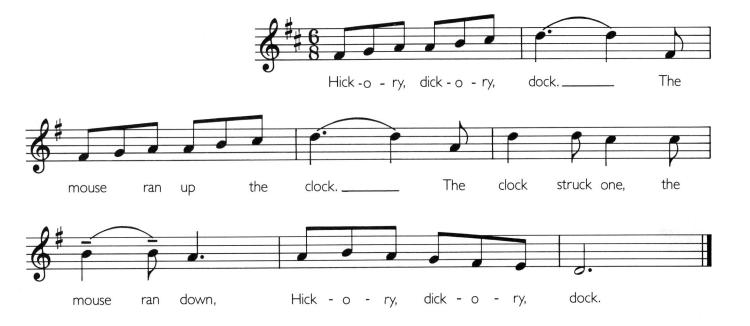

Hick -o - ry, dick -o - ry, dock. _____ The

mouse ran up the clock. _____ The clock struck one, the

mouse ran down, Hick - o - ry, dick - o - ry, dock.

Kum ba yah

traditional

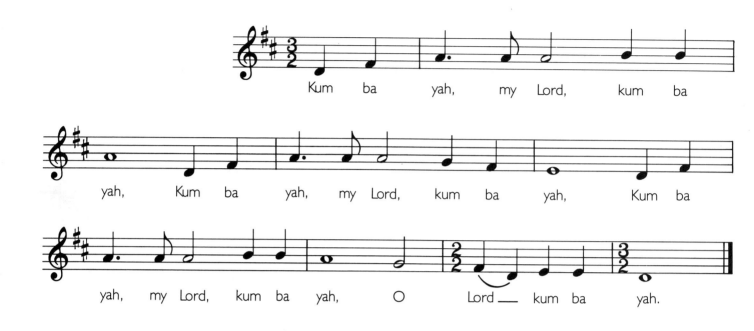

Kum ba yah, my Lord, kum ba yah, Kum ba yah, my Lord, kum ba yah, Kum ba yah, my Lord, kum ba yah, O Lord — kum ba yah.

Three blind mice

traditional

Three blind mice, three blind mice. See how they run, see how they run. — They all ran af - ter the farm - er's wife, who cut off their tails with a car - ving knife, Did you e - ver see such a thing in your life as three blind mice!

The first Nowell

traditional

Puff the magic dragon

Peter Yarrow

Puff the ma - gic dra - gon lived by the sea, And frol - icked in the au - tumn mist in a land called Hon - a - lee. Puff the ma - gic dra - gon lived by the sea, And frol - icked in the au - tumn mist in a land called Hon - a - lee.

An Eriskay love~lilt

Mary MacInness
Collected by Marjory Kennedy-Frazer

When I'm lone - ly, my dear heart, Black the night, or wild the sea, By love's light my foot finds The old path - way to thee.

Funny dance

Peter Davey

Supercalifragilisticexpialidocious

Richard M. Sherman
Robert B. Sherman

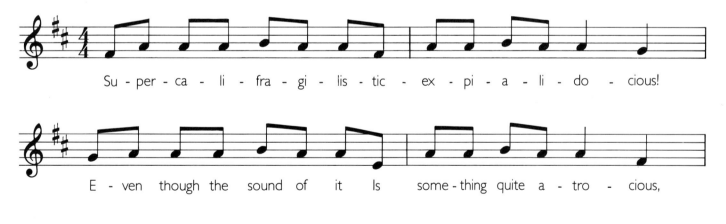

Su - per - ca - li - fra - gi - lis - tic - ex - pi - a - li - do - cious!

E - ven though the sound of it Is some-thing quite a - tro - cious,

If you say it loud e-nough You'll al - ways sound pre - co - cious,

Su - per - ca - li - fra - gi - lis - tic - ex - pi - a - li - do - cious!

Happy birthday to you

M. & P. Hill

Note the new position for the second finger (C natural in this tune).

This new position for the second finger produces F natural on the D string.

Thank U very much

Michael McGear

Jingle bells

traditional

Jin - gle bells, jin - gle bells. jin - gle all the way.

Oh what fun it is to ride in a one horse o - pen sleigh! Oh!

Jin - gle bells, jin - gle bells, jin - gle all the way.

Oh what fun it is to ride in a one horse o - pen sleigh!

Here we go round the mulberry bush

traditional

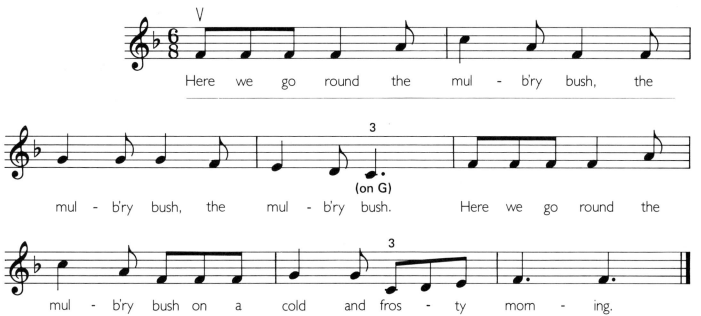

Here we go round the mul - b'ry bush, the

mul - b'ry bush, the mul - b'ry bush. (on G) Here we go round the

mul - b'ry bush on a cold and fros - ty morn - ing.

Folk waltz

Peter Davey

Both positions of second finger in 'Folk Waltz'– F sharp and C natural.
G natural (bar 12) is played with the new position on the E string.

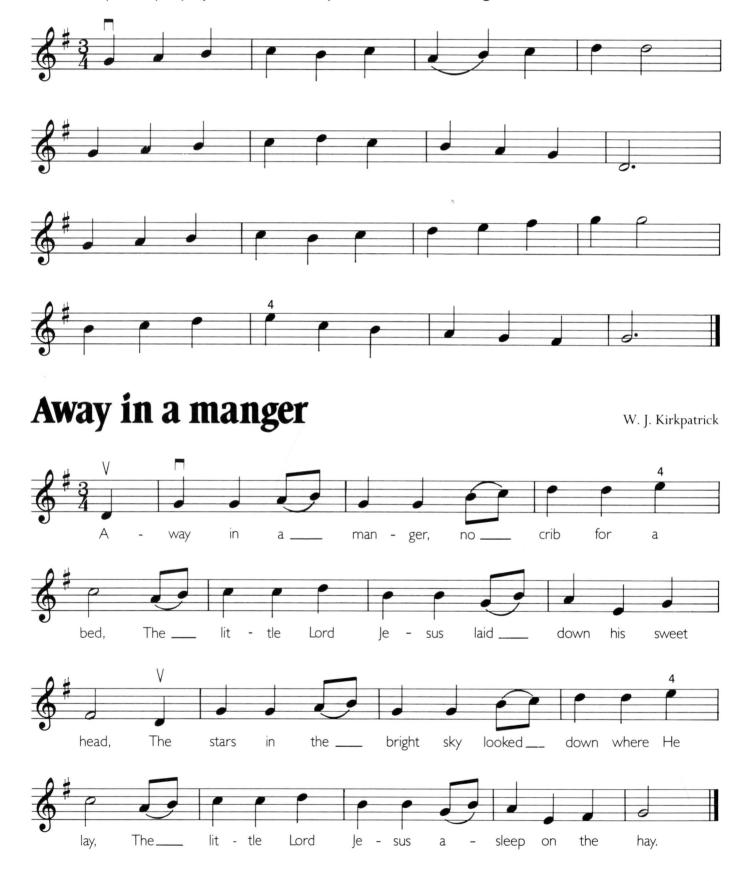

Away in a manger

W. J. Kirkpatrick

A - way in a ___ man - ger, no ___ crib for a bed, The ___ lit - tle Lord Je - sus laid ___ down his sweet head, The stars in the ___ bright sky looked ___ down where He lay, The ___ lit - tle Lord Je - sus a - sleep on the hay.

Now try 'Clown dance' – the teacher's part on page 4.

Morningtown ride

Malvina Reynolds

Train whis - tle blow - ing, Makes a sleep - y noise;
Un - der - neath their blan - kets Go all the girls and boys.
Rock - ing, rol - ling, rid - ing, Out a - long the bay,
All bound for Morn - ing - town, Ma - ny miles a - way.

Last of the summer wine

Ronnie Hazlehurst

While shepherds watched

traditional

*Careful! C natural **and** C sharp!*

While shep - herds watched their flocks by night, All seat - ed on the

ground, The an - gel of the Lord came down and glo - ry shone a - round.

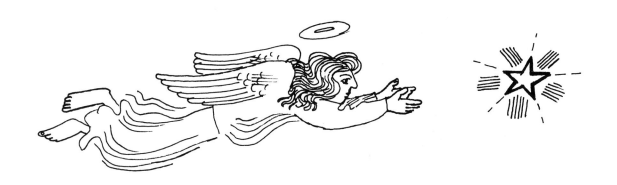

Unto us a boy is born

traditional

Un - to us a boy is born,

King of all cre - a - tion. Came he to a world for - lorn, The

Lord of ev - 'ry na - - - - tion.

Now try playing 'Bobby Shafto' – the teacher's part (page 5).

Theme from the ninth symphony

Beethoven

Morning has broken

words: Eleanor Farjeon
music: Gaelic

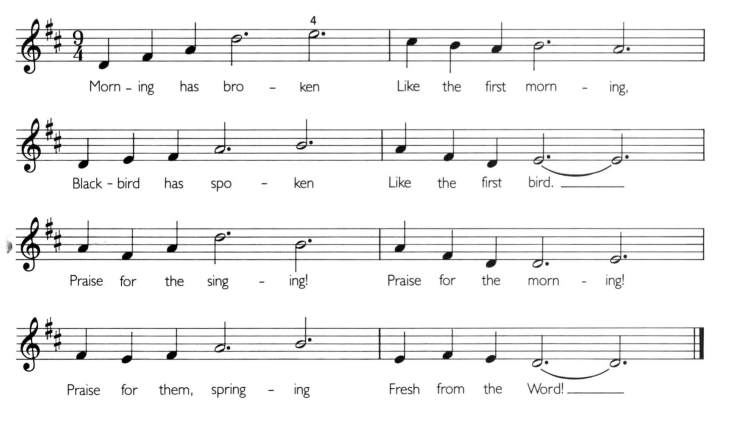

Morn – ing has bro – ken Like the first morn – ing,

Black – bird has spo – ken Like the first bird. _____

Praise for the sing – ing! Praise for the morn – ing!

Praise for them, spring – ing Fresh from the Word! _____

SCALE OF G

God save The Queen

anonymous

1st violin

2nd violin

Plaisir d'amour

G. P. Martini

Plai – sir d'a – mour _____ ne du – re qu'un ___ mo – ment. _____ Cha – grin d'a – mour du – re toute ___ la vie. _____

Deck the hall

traditional Welsh

Deck the hall with boughs of hol – ly, Fa – la – la – la – la, Fa – la – la – la. 'Tis the sea – son to be jol – ly, Fa – la – la – la – la, Fa – la – la – la. Fill the mead cup, drain the bar – rel, Fa – la – la – la – la, la – la – la. Troll the an – cient Christ – mas ca – rol, Fa – la – la – la – la, Fa – la – la – la.

Sing a song of sixpence

traditional

Watch out for the change of key at the beginning of verse 2!

Sing a song of sixpence,
A pocket full of rye,
Four and twenty blackbirds
Baked in a pie.
When the pie was opened
The birds began to sing;
Wasn't that a dainty dish
To set before the king!

The king was in his counting-house,
Counting out his money,
The queen was in the parlour,
Eating bread and honey,
The maid was in the garden,
Hanging out the clothes,
When down came a blackbird
And pecked off her nose.

Theme from 'Swallow Suite'

Peter Davey

My love is like a red, red rose

Robert Burns

Oh, my love is like a red, red rose that's new – ly sprung in June. Oh, ____ my love is like the me – lo – dy that's sweet – ly played in tune. _____ As fair art thou, my bon – nie lass, so deep in love am I _____ And I will love thee still, my dear, till all the seas go dry. _____

The grand old Duke of York

traditional

Give me oil in my lamp

traditional

Theme from 'Bridges of Paris'

Peter Davey

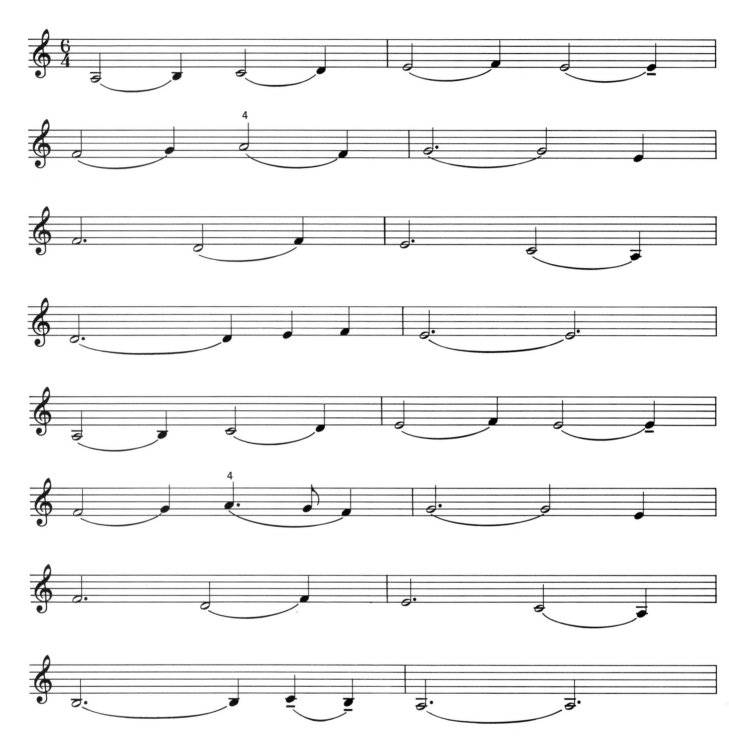

Brother James' air

J. L. M. Bain

New position for third finger — C sharp on the G string.

Hornpipe

Peter Davey

DC – go back to the beginning and play without repeating to end at FINE.

Try 'Au clair de la lune', the teacher's part on page 6.

O soldier, soldier

traditional

'Oh sol – dier, sol – dier, won't you mar – ry me? With your mus – ket, fife and drum.' 'Oh no, sweet maid, I can-not mar-ry thee for I have no coat to put on.' Then off she went to her grand – fa-ther's chest and got him a coat of the ve – ry, ve – ry best, She got him a coat of the ve – ry, ve-ry best and the sol – dier put it ___ on. 'Oh sol – dier, sol – dier, won't you mar-ry me? With your mus – ket, .fife and drum.' 'Oh no, sweet maid, I can – not mar – ry thee for I have a wife of my own.'

SCALE OF A

Scottish medley

You could play 'My Love is like a red, red rose' (page 38), then continue with these two tunes.

SOLDIER'S JOY

(FINE)

WHITE COCKADE

DC 'Soldier's Joy'

French folk medley

ALOUETTE

AUPRES DE MA BLONDE

The birdcatcher's song

Mozart

St Anthony chorale

Haydn (attributed)

(2nd violin)

Acknowledgements

The following copyright owners have kindly granted their permission for the inclusion of these items:

Boosey and Hawkes Music Publishers Ltd for 'An Eriskay love lilt', sung by Mary MacInnes. Collected by Marjory Kennedy-Fraser © 1909 Boosey & Co Ltd (Reprinted from 'Songs of the Hebrides' by permission of the Estate of M. Kennedy-Fraser and Boosey & Hawkes Music Publishers Ltd).

Campbell Connelly & Co Ltd for 'Supercalifragilisticexpialidocious' by Richard M. Sherman and Robert B. Sherman © 1963 Wonderland Music Co Inc. Reproduced by permission of Campbell Connelly & Co Ltd, 8-9 Frith Street, London W1V 5TZ.

Chappell Music Ltd and International Music Publications Ltd for 'Little Donkey' by Eric Boswell © 1959 Warner/Chappell Music Ltd, London W6 8BS. Reproduced by permission of International Music Publications Ltd.

Peter Davey for 'Folk waltz', 'Funny dance', 'Hello morning', 'Hornpipe', 'Off to France in the morning', 'One finger dance', 'Rolling', 'Seagull', 'Spinning wheel', 'Summer shine', 'Theme from Bridges of Paris', 'Theme from Swallow Suite', 'Waltz' and 'Windmill song'.

Noel Gay Music Co Ltd for 'Thank U very much' by Michael McGear © 1967 by Noel Gay Music Co Ltd 8-9 Frith Street, London W1V 5TZ. All rights reserved. Used by Permission.

Ronnie Hazlehurst for 'Last of the summer wine' © Ronnie Hazlehurst Ms.

David Higham Associates Ltd for the words of 'Morning has broken' by Eleanor Farjeon from 'The Children's Bells' published by Oxford University Press © 1931 Published by Oxford University Press.

International Music Publications for 'I'm the Urban Spaceman' by Neil Innes © 1968 EMI Music Publishing Ltd, London WC2H 0EA. Reproduced by permission of International Music Publications.

Leosong Copyright Service Ltd for 'Morningtown Ride' by Malvina Reynolds © 1959 Amadeo-Brio Music Inc. International Copyright Secured. Administered by Leosong Copyright Service Ltd.

Oxford University Press for the words of 'Andrew mine, Jasper mine', words by C K Offer from 'Three Moravian Carols' © 1962 Oxford University Press. Used by permission.

Keith Prowse Music Pub Co Ltd for 'Happy Birthday to you' words and music by Patty S. Hill and Mildred Hill © 1935 (Renewed 1962) Summy-Birchard Inc, USA, Keith Prowse Music Pub Co Ltd, London WC2H 0EA. Reproduced by permission of International Music Publications.

Warner Chappell Music Ltd/ Cherry Lane Publishing/ International Music Publications Ltd for 'Puff the magic dragon', words and music by Peter Yarrow and Leonard Lipton © 1963 Pepamar Music Corp/ WB Music Corp, USA/ Honalee Melodies/ Cherry Lane Publishing, 70% Warner/ Chappell Music Ltd, London W6 8BS. Reproduced by permission of International Music Publications.

Every effort has been made to trace and acknowledge copyright owners. If any right has been omitted the publishers offer their apologies and will rectify this in subsequent editions following notification.

The inside illustrations are by Bernard Cheese.
The cover is by Alex Ayliffe.
The end-paper drawings are by Kevin Maddison.

The publishers would like to thank David Bass and Jill Townsend for their help in the preparation of this book.

Printed in Great Britain by Caligraving Ltd, Thetford, Norfolk.

Index of titles

Alouette, 44
Andrew mine, Jasper mine, 11
Au clair de la lune, 6, 14
Auprès de ma blonde, 44
Away in a manger, 30

Baa, baa, black sheep, 21, 22
Big Ben, 15
Birdcatcher's song, The, 45
Bobby Shafto, 5
Brother James' air, 40

Can-can, 23
Clown dance, 4, 10, 21

Deck the hall, 35

Eriskay love-lilt, An, 26

First Nowell, The, 25
Folk waltz, 30
French folk medley, 44
Frère Jacques, 8, 20
Funny dance, 27

Give me oil in my lamp, 39
God save The Queen, 34
Grand old Duke of York, The, 39

Happy birthday to you, 28
Hello morning, 14
Here we go round the mulberry bush, 29
Hickory dickory dock, 23
Hornpipe, 41
Hot cross buns, 8, 16
Hush-a-bye baby, 13

I'm the urban spaceman, 16

Jingle bells, 29

Kum ba yah, 24

Last of the summer wine, 31
Little bird, 10, 18
Little donkey, 19
London Bridge, 17
London's burning, 23

Morning has broken, 33
Morningtown ride, 31
My love is like a red, red rose, 38

Off to France in the morning, 22
One finger dance, 7
Oranges and lemons, 16
O soldier, soldier, 42

Plaisir d'amour, 35
Puff the magic dragon, 26

Rolling, 12

St Anthony Chorale, 46
Seagull, 7
Scottish medley, 43
Shepherd's hey, 14
Sing a song of sixpence, 36
Soldier's joy, 43
Spinning wheel, 7
Summer shine, 11
Suo-gân, 9
Supercalifragilisticexpialidocious, 27

Thank U very much, 28
Theme from 'Swallow Suite', 37
Theme from 'Bridges of Paris', 40
Theme from the ninth symphony, 33
Three blind mice, 24
Twinkle, twinkle little star, 13, 18

Unto us a boy is born, 32

Waltz, 9
When the saints go marching in, 12
While shepherds watched their flocks by night, 32
White cockade, 43
Windmill song, 9
Winds through the olive trees, 20

More music books from A & C Black . . .

Abracadabra Cello
0 7136 5637 9

Abracadabra Viola
0 7136 5629 8

Two perfect books for pupil and teacher; wide-ranging selections of songs and tunes, carefully graded to cover each aspect of technique for the beginner.

Fourteen Hymns and Songs
0 7136 3234 8

Favourite songs for assembly, arranged simply and flexibly for beginner ensembles. The melodies can be played or sung, and accompanied by a range of easy parts for recorders, tuned and untuned percussion, strings, guitars and B♭ instruments, played singly or in any combination.

For details of other music books write to A & C Black, P.O. Box 19, Huntingdon, Cambs PE19 3SF

8765